BEACHCOMBING
exploring the seashore

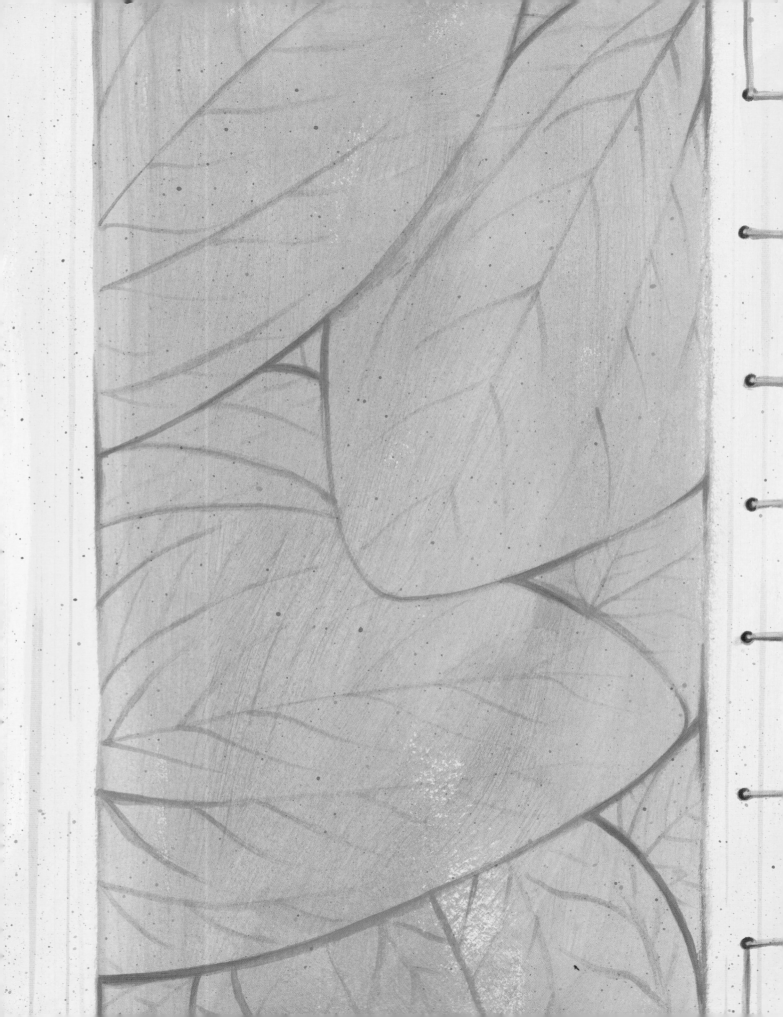

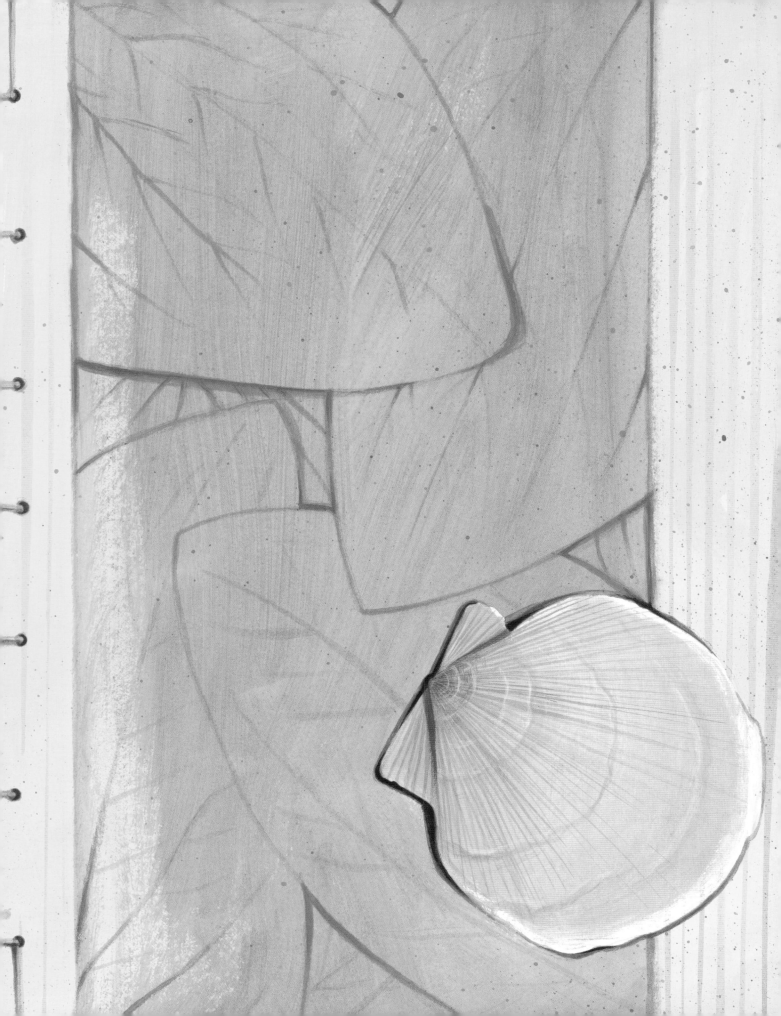

To Joyce

PUFFIN BOOKS
Published by the Penguin Group
Penguin Group (USA) LLC
375 Hudson Street
New York, New York 10014

USA * Canada * UK * Ireland * Australia
New Zealand * India * South Africa * China

penguin.com
A Penguin Random House Company

First published in the United States of America by Dutton Children's Books,
a division of Penguin Young Readers Group, 2004
Published by Puffin Books, an imprint of Penguin Young Readers Group, 2014

THE LIBRARY OF CONGRESS HAS CATALOGED THE DUTTON CHILDREN'S BOOKS EDITION AS FOLLOWS:
Arnosky, Jim.
Beachcombing / by Jim Arnosky. 1st ed. p. cm
Summary: Illustrations and text describe some of the many things that can be found on a walk along a beach,
including coconuts, shark teeth, jellyfish, crabs, and different kinds of shells.
ISBN 978-0-525-47104-2 (hardcover)
1. Seashore biology—Juvenile literature. 2. Beachcombing—Juvenile literature.
[1. Beachcombing. 2. Seashore ecology. 3. Ecology.] 1. Title.
QH95.7.A76 2004
578.769'9—dc22 2003062484

Puffin Books ISBN 978-0-14-751163-8

Manufactured in China

1 3 5 7 9 10 8 6 4 2

BEACHCOMBING

exploring the seashore

by Jim Arnosky

PUFFIN BOOKS

AN IMPRINT OF PENGUIN GROUP (USA)

*B*eachcombing is walking slowly near the ocean, looking for bits and pieces of nature the waves wash in.

It is wading ankle-deep in the foamy surf and pretending that you're all alone on your very own tropical island.

The Complete Beachcomber

To be a beachcomber, all you need is sunblock (with an SPF of 30 or higher), a broad-brimmed hat to shade your head, sunglasses to protect your eyes, and a bucket to carry shells and other treasures you find.

SEASHELLS

Beachcombing is collecting colorful seashells and learning all their names. Remember, each and every seashell once housed a marine animal. Collect only empty shells. If you find any shells that are still inhabited, return them to the water.

Cockleshell

Slipper

Calico Clam

Mussel

Worm Shell

Whelk

Olive

Tulip

Cardita

Sea Urchin

Razor Clam

Pen

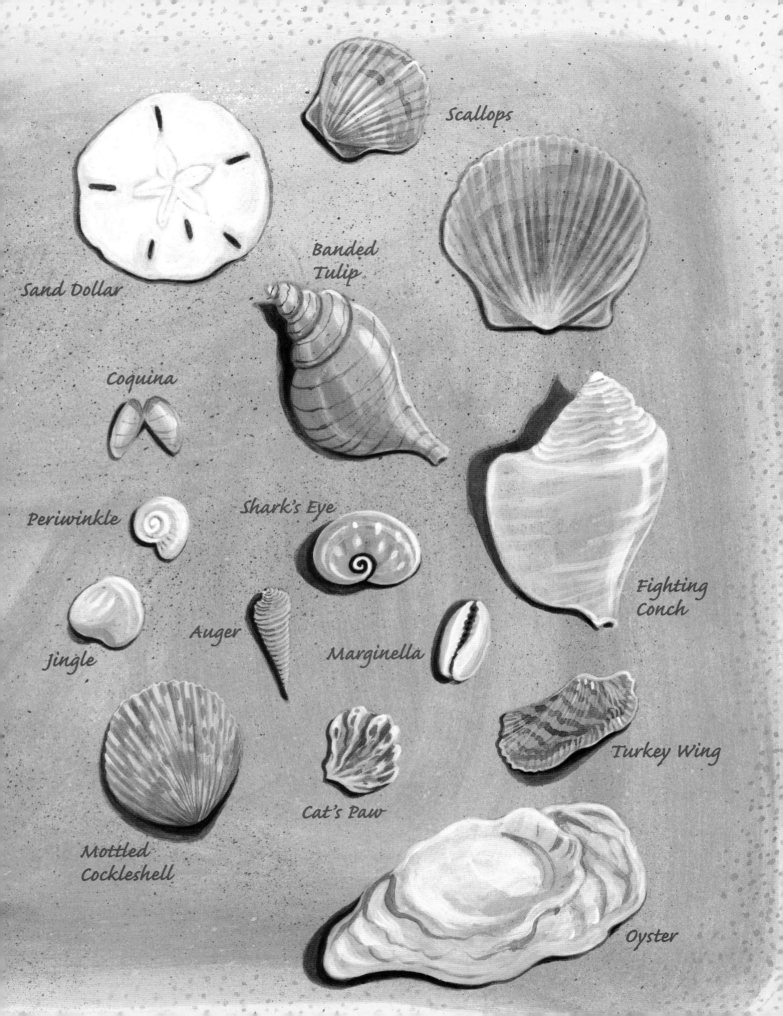

Scallops

Sand Dollar

Banded
Tulip

Coquina

Periwinkle

Shark's Eye

Fighting
Conch

Jingle

Auger

Marginella

Turkey Wing

Mottled
Cockleshell

Cat's Paw

Oyster

CRABS

Among the galaxy of seashells strewn along the shoreline, you may find broken bits and pieces of crab
shells. If you are lucky, you will find an entire crab
shell, complete with legs attached, recently
shed by a living crab.

crab claw

crab carapace

shed intact shell

Watch for live crabs in the water.
Living crabs such as this Blue Crab
will pinch you if you accidentally
step on them.

Blue Crab

Hermit Crab

Hermit Crabs inhabit the empty
shells of other creatures. This
Hermit Crab is living inside the
abandoned shell of a Banded
Tulip Snail.

On beaches left exposed by low tide, you might see tiny crabs scurrying out of their holes, foraging for bits of food. The small pale-yellow crabs are Ghost Crabs. The darker, purplish crabs are Fiddler Crabs, named for their one large claw that resembles a violin or fiddle being held high.

Ghost Crab

Fiddler Crab

When you see a Ghost Crab or Fiddler Crab, sit quietly and watch for more. Soon you will be surrounded by tiny crabs venturing out of their holes.

Many species of crabs can be identified by shape alone. Here are eight crab shapes to look for in the water or on the beach.

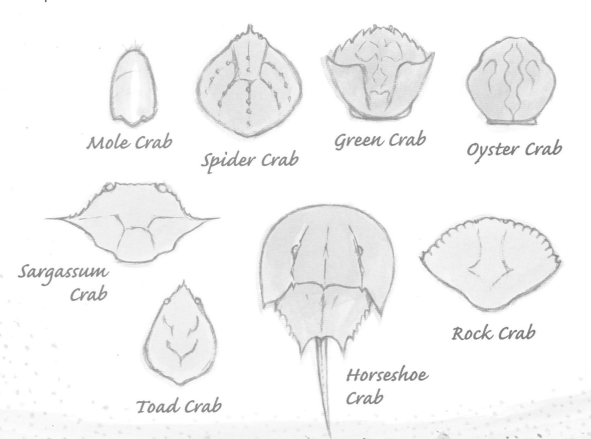

Mole Crab

Spider Crab

Green Crab

Oyster Crab

Sargassum Crab

Toad Crab

Horseshoe Crab

Rock Crab

HORSESHOE CRAB

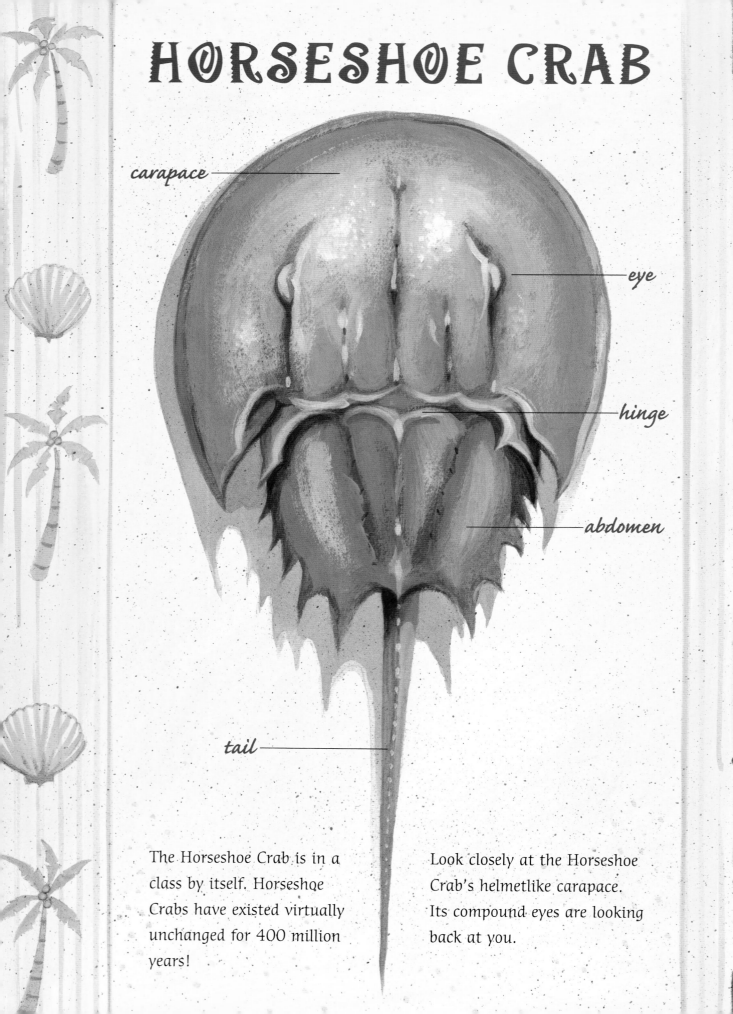

carapace

eye

hinge

abdomen

tail

The Horseshoe Crab is in a class by itself. Horseshoe Crabs have existed virtually unchanged for 400 million years!

Look closely at the Horseshoe Crab's helmetlike carapace. Its compound eyes are looking back at you.

The Horseshoe Crab is the biggest crab a beachcomber is likely to find. It doesn't pinch like other crabs. It is okay to gently flip one over with your toe to see the underside. Just make sure you gently flip it back the way it was.

Like all crabs, Horseshoe Crabs shed their shells to grow. Finding a shed shell that's intact is something special. Finding the shed shell of a baby Horseshoe Crab is a treasure.

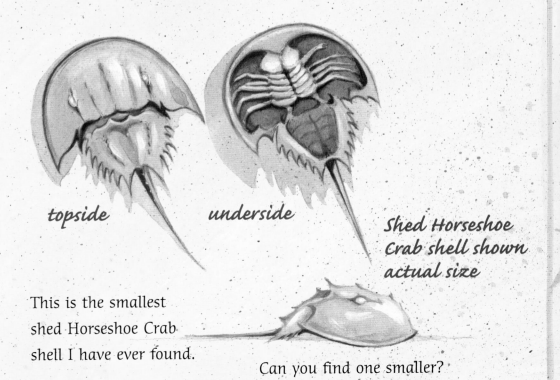

topside   underside

Shed Horseshoe
Crab shell shown
actual size

This is the smallest
shed Horseshoe Crab
shell I have ever found.

Can you find one smaller?

What are those ghostly, gooey-looking forms on the wet sand? They are jellyfish, washed in and stranded by the tide. I never step on stranded jellyfish. Nor will I touch them with my hands. Many species of jellyfish can sting.

I do enjoy looking at them, and I try to sketch the shape of every one I see. Here are some of the jellyfish shapes I found one morning on one beach.

Portuguese Man-of-War and seaweed

Occasionally, Portuguese Man-of-War jellyfish will wash ashore. A sting from the tentacles of this sea creature can be very painful. Man-of-War jellyfish are easy to identify. They look like little blue balloons. If you see one on the sand or tangled in seaweed, stay away! Even the tiniest Man-of-War jellyfish has long tentacles that can sting you.

In the water, a Man-of-War jellyfish floats on the surface with its long, food-catching tentacles hanging down.

A CORAL BEACH

Wherever there is a coral reef offshore, the beach will be bright white, because it is made up entirely of broken bits of sun-bleached coral.

Beachcombers on coral beaches have to wear wading shoes or sneakers to protect their feet from sharp pieces of coral.

Even the large boulders you see on a coral beach are actually chunks of fossilized coral reef. Look closely at coral beach boulders and you will see the different shapes and patterns of coral species that once lived out on the reef.

Besides seashells and crab shells, there are things unique to a coral sea that wash up on the beach. Here are some of the more unusual things beachcombers can find on a coral beach.

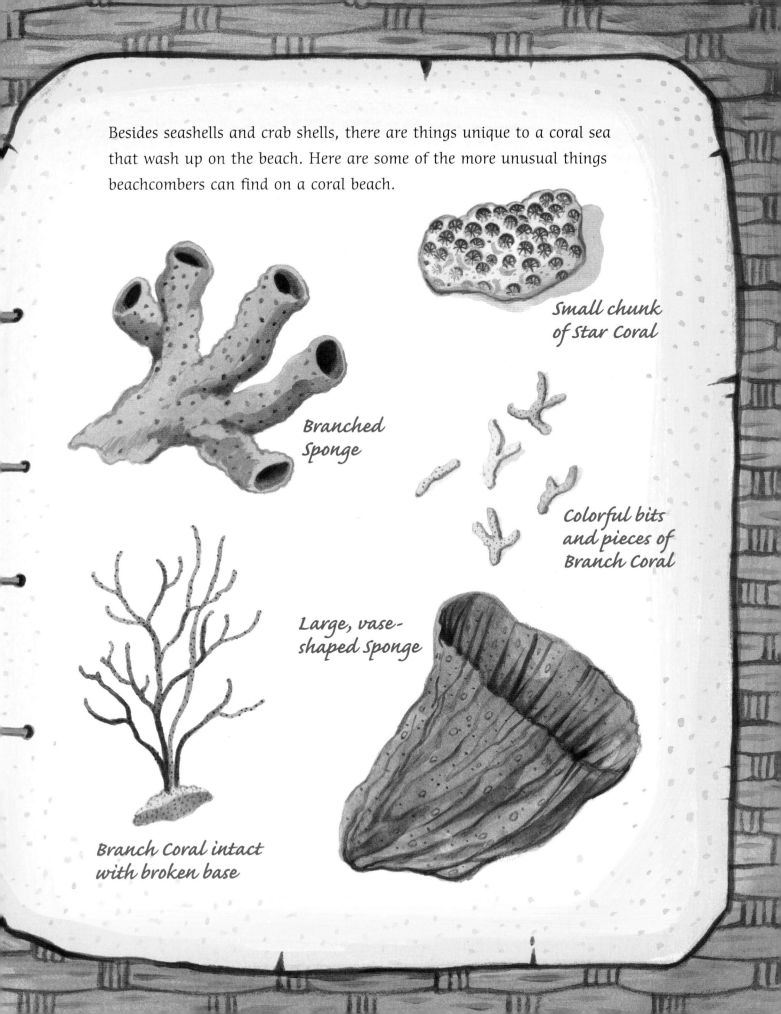

Small chunk of Star Coral

Branched Sponge

Colorful bits and pieces of Branch Coral

Large, vase-shaped Sponge

Branch Coral intact with broken base

WHERE DO COCONUTS COME FROM?

Question: *Where do coconuts come from?*
Answer: *Palm trees.*

Question: *Where do palm trees come from?*
Answer: *Coconuts.*

Beachcombers occasionally find coconuts washed ashore. Almost all have floated a great distance from some faraway place.

Every coconut you see onshore has fallen from a palm tree somewhere. And every palm tree growing on the beach has sprouted from a coconut that once washed ashore.

This is a newly sprouted coconut palm. If the waves don't unearth it and the wind doesn't blow it away, it will grow to be a magnificent shoreline tree.

Where do coconut pirates come from?
I have no idea!

BEACH BIRDS

A beachcomber's constant companions are the ever-present beach birds. Beach birds search the wet beach for freshly washed-in bits of food, such as tiny crabs or shellfish.

Sandpipers, small and large, run from wave wash to wave wash to catch crabs burrowing into the wet sand. Sandpipers will walk behind or ahead of you, always keeping just enough distance from you to feel safe.

Sandpipers come in sizes that range from short and small to big and tall. All species of sandpipers are mottled brown or gray in color.

Of all the birds on the beach, my favorites are the gulls, terns, and skimmers. Gulls are the boldest of birds. Wherever a gull lands, it makes the place its own. I admire that. Terns glide on the wind over the waves so gracefully, they make me wish I could do it with them. And I love watching Black Skimmers speed along, using their long bills to slice through the water surface and snap up small fish.

Herring Gull

Ring-billed Gull

Common Tern

Laughing Gull

Royal Tern

Black Skimmer

SOME SPECIAL FINDS

This is the egg case of a skate, also known as a Mermaid's Purse.

Whelk egg cases in a chain

Walk the length of a beach one way. Then turn and walk back, looking down at the very same spots. The view from the opposite direction always reveals something you missed before.

This is when a beachcomber finds the most unexpected treasures, such as Mermaid's Purses and Sea Beans.

Depending on the size of the individual whelk they came from, these chainlike egg cases can be up to ten times larger than the one pictured here.

Mermaid's Purses are actually the leathery egg cases of either stingrays, skates, or sharks. Collect only those that are empty and hard. Any that are soft and still have contents should be put back into the water.

Other curious-looking egg cases you may find are those of whelks and conchs. These egg cases resemble extra-long rattlesnake rattles. When thoroughly dried, they rattle when shaken.

Sea Beans look a lot like large, flattened chestnuts. They are the seeds of trees that grow along the banks of the Amazon River in South America. Because they're as beautiful as they are rare and have drifted such great distances, Sea Beans are highly prized by beachcombers.

Sea Beans shown actual size

Sea Beans can be flat or round.

This curious-looking thing is actually a small coconut.

Broken tooth or tusk

SHARK TEETH

Most of the shark teeth we see are the big, scary-looking ones in the mouths of sharks on TV or in plastic replicas of huge sharks on display in restaurants and museums. However, sharks come in all sizes, and so do shark teeth.

Sharks have been swimming in the oceans for millions of years. In all that time, they have changed very little. The fossilized teeth of ancient shark species are similar to the teeth of sharks alive today.

Where the beach sand is dark gray in color and peppered with lots of black grit, the beach is most likely fossiliferous. Some of the black bits in the sand could be fossilized shark teeth!

Tooth of a living Great White Shark

Tooth of a living Mako Shark

SHARK EXHIBIT

This model shows a Great White Shark ready to bite. Sometimes when a shark bites, a tooth breaks off and sinks to the bottom of the ocean. Those that wash ashore are found by beach-combers.

Scoop a handful of wet sand and search through the broken shells and sand pebbles for tiny fossilized shark teeth. Here is one morning's gleanings of shark teeth on a famously fossiliferous Gulf Coast beach.

All of these teeth are shown actual size.

Some of the teeth you find will be brown. These are also fossils.

This large piece is not a shark tooth. It is a fossilized bone.

Whose bone? We don't know. It is not a shark bone. Sharks do not have bones. Their skeletons are all cartilage.

Finding a pure white tooth from a living shark, such as this large Tiger Shark tooth, is extremely rare. Most shark teeth you find will be fossilized and black or gray in color.

The beach is one place that is new every day.
The tide washes in, and it washes away.

A beachcomber can walk the same beach again and
again and always find something new and wonderful.

Author's Note

To research this book, my wife, Deanna, and I visited twenty-six different beaches along the Atlantic and Gulf coasts. We walked the shorelines looking for things that made each beach special—the color of the sand, the condition of the washed-in shells, and the variety of shorebirds. And when we had walked as far as we wanted to go in one direction, we turned and followed our own footprints back to where we had started. We sat and watched the ocean for the splashes of fish and the distant shapes of boats. We waded ankle-deep in the waves. It was wonderful!

I made lots of little sketches in my notebook. We took pictures of everything, even our own footprints in the sand. When we got back home again, I used my sketches and photographs to create the paintings in *Beachcombing*. I hope this book helps you to enjoy your visits to the seashore—real or imagined—as much as we have enjoyed ours.

Jim Arnosky

More Books for Beachcombers and Naturalists

Arnosky, Jim. *All About Sharks*. New York: Scholastic, 2003.

——. *Field Trips: Bug Hunting, Animal Tracking, Bird-watching, Shore Walking*. New York: HarperCollins, 2002.

Arthur, Alex. *Eyewitness: Shell*. New York: DK Publishing, 2000.

Berger, Melvin, and Gilda Berger. *What Makes an Ocean Wave? Questions and Answers About Oceans and Ocean Life*. New York: Scholastic Reference, 2001.

Cerullo, Mary M. *The Truth About Dangerous Sea Creatures*. San Francisco: Chronicle Books, 2003.

Davies, Nicola. *Surprising Sharks*. Boston: Candlewick, 2003.

George, Twig. *Jellies*. Brookfield, CT: Millbrook Press, 2001.

Greenaway, Theresa. *The Secret World of Crabs*. Austin, TX: Raintree/Steck-Vaughn, 2001.

Parker, Steve. *Eyewitness: Seashore*. New York: DK Publishing, 2000.

Rustad, Martha E. H., and Jody Rake. *Jellyfish*. Mankato, MN: Pebble Books, 2003.

Sharth, Sharon. *Sea Jellies: From Corals to Jellyfish*. Danbury, CT: Franklin Watts, 2002.

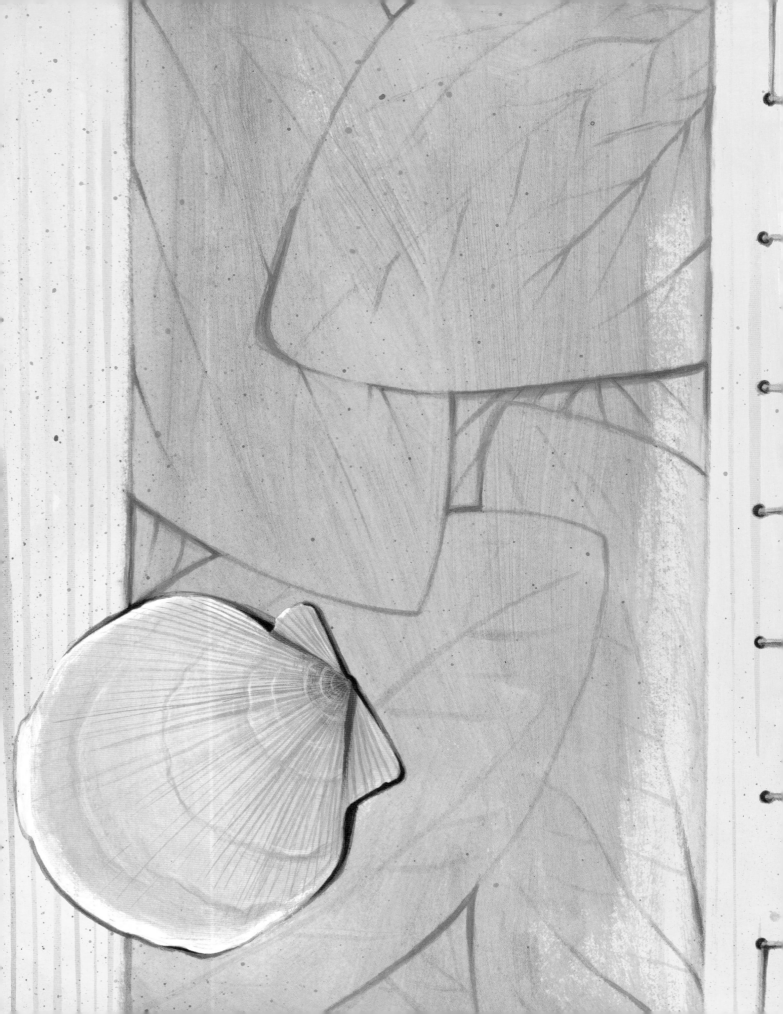

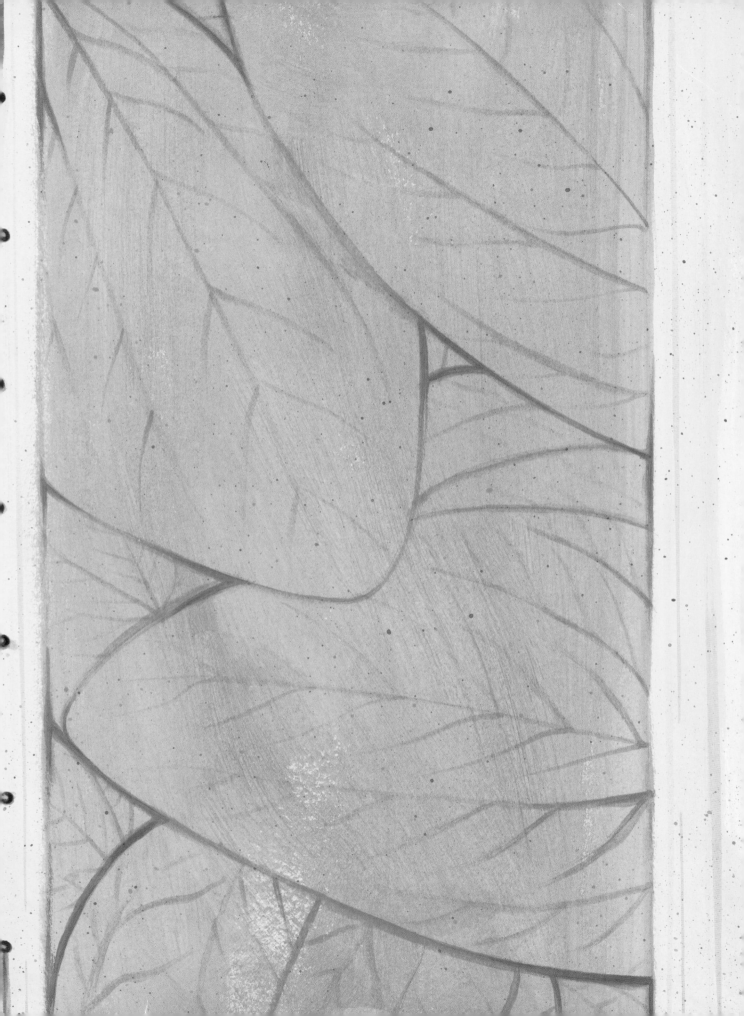

Jim Arnosky

is the award-winning author and illustrator of many books for children, including *Armadillo's Orange.* He wrote *Beachcombing* while living in a camper called "Leeky Teeky" in the Florida Keys.

Mr. Arnosky spends most of his time studying plants and animals on a fifty-two-acre farm in Vermont, where he lives with his wife, Deanna.

Visit him online at www.jimarnosky.com.